Wendorff, Anne
ATOS BL 3.1
Points: 0.5

LG

DOG BREEDS

Shetland Sheepdogs

by Anne Wendorff

Consultant:
Michael Leuthner, D.V.M.
PetCare Clinic, Madison, Wisc.

BLASTOFF! READERS 4

BELLWETHER MEDIA · MINNEAPOLIS, MN

Note to Librarians, Teachers, and Parents:

Blastoff! Readers are carefully developed by literacy experts and combine standards-based content with developmentally appropriate text.

Level 1 provides the most support through repetition of high-frequency words, light text, predictable sentence patterns, and strong visual support.

Level 2 offers early readers a bit more challenge through varied simple sentences, increased text load, and less repetition of high-frequency words.

Level 3 advances early-fluent readers toward fluency through increased text and concept load, less reliance on visuals, longer sentences, and more literary language.

Level 4 builds reading stamina by providing more text per page, increased use of punctuation, greater variation in sentence patterns, and increasingly challenging vocabulary.

Level 5 encourages children to move from "learning to read" to "reading to learn" by providing even more text, varied writing styles, and less familiar topics.

Whichever book is right for your reader, Blastoff! Readers are the perfect books to build confidence and encourage a love of reading that will last a lifetime!

This edition first published in 2010 by Bellwether Media, Inc.

Library of Congress Cataloging-in-Publication Data
Wendorff, Anne.
  Shetland sheepdogs / by Anne Wendorff.
    p. cm. – (Blastoff! readers. Dog breeds)
Includes bibliographical references and index.
  Summary: "Simple text and full-color photography introduce beginning readers to the characteristics of the dog breed Shetland sheepdogs. Developed by literacy experts for students in kindergarten through third grade"–Provided by publisher.
  ISBN 978-1-60014-302-1 (hardcover : alk. paper)
  1. Shetland sheepdog–Juvenile literature. I. Title.
SF429.S62W46 2010
636.737–dc22
                              2009037211

Printed in the United States of America, North Mankato, MN.
010110   1149

Contents

What Are Shetland Sheepdogs?

Shetland Sheepdogs are a strong, smart **breed** of dog. They are **herding dogs**. They are also called Shelties. Shelties are 13 to 16 inches (33 to 40.6 centimeters) tall. They weigh 14 to 27 pounds (6.5 to 12.3 kilograms). Their tails are long and straight. They also have long **muzzles**.

Shelties have two layers of hair. The outer layer of hair is long and rough. The inner layer of hair is short and thick.

Shelties are black, brown, or blue-gray.
They **shed** their hair during the fall
and spring. They often have tan or
white **markings**.

! fun fact

A Sheltie's outer layer of
hair keeps it warm and
dry in cold, wet weather.

History of Shetland Sheepdogs

Shelties are from the Shetland Islands. The Shetland Islands are north of Scotland. Shelties are named after the islands. Farmers bred Border Collies with small, long-haired dogs to create Shelties. They were bred to help farmers herd animals.

Shelties worked on farms until people visiting the islands decided to make them pets. Pet Shelties were brought to England and America in the 1800s. The **American Kennel Club (AKC)** declared Shelties an official dog breed in 1911.

Shetland Sheepdogs Today

Shelties compete against other herding dogs in dog shows. They are judged on how they look and act during the competition.

Shelties also compete in obedience events, herding events, and tracking events. Shelties are good at these events because they are smart and easy to train.

Shelties also like to compete in **agility**.
They like to jump over hurdles and run
through tunnels.

Shelties are good at agility because they are smart and athletic. Competing in agility exercises a Sheltie's mind and body.

Shelties are good **guard dogs**. They often bark at other animals or people. Barking helps Shelties herd animals.

They also bark to tell their owners that a
stranger is nearby. They usually do not like
new people and are protective of their owners.

Shelties are often trained to be **working dogs**. Working dogs do jobs to help people. A seeing eye dog is a working dog for someone who is blind. Shelties make good working dogs because they are loyal and obedient.

Shelties are friendly around kids and adults. They must be kept active if kept as pets. They love to play fetch with balls and Frisbees.

Shelties enjoy games and activities that challenge them. They are always eager to please their owners!

Glossary

agility—a sport where dogs run through a series of obstacles

American Kennel Club (AKC)—a group that monitors and promotes purebred dogs

breed—a type of dog

guard dog—a dog that barks or alerts its owner when strangers are near

herding dogs—dogs that move animals from place to place for humans

markings—patterns of color in a dog's hair

muzzle—the nose, jaws, and mouth of an animal

shed—to lose hair

working dog—a dog that does a job to help people

To Learn More

AT THE LIBRARY

Miller, Marie-Therese. *Hunting and Herding Dogs*. New York, N.Y.: Chelsea Clubhouse, 2007.

Stone, Lynn. *Shetland Sheepdogs*. New York, N.Y.: Rourke Publishing, 2006.

Tatro, Brenda. *Rowdy: The Sheltie*. Bloomington, Ind.: Trafford Publishing, 2003.

ON THE WEB

Learning more about Shetland Sheepdogs is as easy as 1, 2, 3.

1. Go to www.factsurfer.com.

2. Enter "Shetland Sheepdogs" into the search box.

3. Click the "Surf" button and you will see a list of related Web sites.

With factsurfer.com, finding more information is just a click away.

Index

The images in this book are reproduced through the courtesy of: Ruth Ann Johnston, front cover; J. Harriosn/Kimballstock, pp. 4-5; Nick Dronoff-Guthrie, pp. 6, 10, 13, 14, 15; Mark Raycraft, pp. 7, 12; Ron Kimball/Kimballstock, p. 8; Jon Eppard, p. 9; Juniors Bildarchiv, pp. 11, 17, 21; ARCO/P. Wegner, p. 16; Wong Chee Yen, pp. 18-19; Rick Wilking, p. 19; Michael Krabs, p. 20.